ROSEMARY VEREY'S GARDEN DIARY

Rosemary Verey is a renowned plantswoman and one of England's foremost gardening writers. For the last thirty years she has gardened at Barnsley House in Gloucestershire, creating a garden that is an inspiration in all seasons for its blend of first-class design and superb plantsmanship. She is the author of a number of classic works including *The Art of Planting*, *The Garden in Winter* and *The Countrywoman's Year*.

ROSEMARY VEREY'S GARDEN DIARY

LITTLE, BROWN AND COMPANY
BOSTON · TORONTO · LONDON

First American Edition

ISBN 0-316-89979-8

2 4 6 8 10 9 7 5 3 1

Published simultaneously in Canada by Little, Brown & Company (Canada) Limited

Printed in Hong Kong

Half-title page illustration: *Anemone* 'Honorine Jobert'
Title page illustration: *Kolkwitzia amabilis* and *Paeonia lactiflora* 'Ballerina'

INTRODUCTION

Some people make a habit of sitting down each evening to record the day's happenings in their diaries. It becomes automatic and, for a gardener, it is invaluable when, years later, you cannot conjure up a memorable garden visit or the name of a special plant. So why not keep your own book of gardening days?

When, thirty years ago, I first started planning my garden and buying trees and shrubs in earnest, it was easy to keep facts and ideas in my head. I soon came to realize, however, that I needed a record – perhaps a reminder of the clematis now climbing through the golden privet or of the garden where I had seen a wonderful herbaceous border. On the more practical side it was useful to turn up how many seed potatoes were ordered last year and when seeds were sown, both indoors and out.

'A Gard'ners work is never at an end; it begins with the year, and continues to the next; he prepares the ground, and then he sows it; after that he plants, and then he gathers the fruits,' John Evelyn wrote in the introduction to his *Kalendarium Hortense*, first published in 1664. He compiled this calendar in the 1650s for his own use and as a seasonal reminder for his gardener at Sayes Court, in Deptford, London. Each month he describes what is to be

done in the Orchard and Olitory (Kitchen) Garden, in the Parterre and Flower Garden, and tells which fruits and flowers are in their prime. Such was the interest in gardening that ten editions of Evelyn's *Kalendar* were published until the final edition of 1706.

Richard Bradley's *Gentlemen and Gardeners Kalendar* appeared in 1718. Bradley, the first Professor of Botany at Cambridge, had, as he said, 'a passion for gardening'. He was in the habit of noting in a journal whatever he 'found remarkable in gardening whether in Britain, or other parts of Europe'. His book remained a favourite until superseded by Philip Miller's *The Gardeners' Kalendar* which went into sixteen editions between 1731 and 1775. What is remarkable is the greatly increased number of flowers he mentioned compared with those available in John Evelyn's time.

The tradition of these garden calendars has continued until today, their popularity waxing and waning with fashion. They all follow the same pattern – to instruct and advise. To garden historians today they are invaluable as a record of plants and planting as well as in throwing light on contemporary fashions in garden design. My book of days is a more humble affair, with seasonal suggestions and beautiful pictures. These I hope will inspire garden owners to record their own ideas, ambitions and planting plans.

In 1962 I started keeping my first gardening diary – more of a scrapbook really – and now it makes fascinating reading. It began as a record of the plants we had bought, their provenance, where they were planted, sometimes what they had cost. As the years went by the information became more detailed, with notes about gardens we visited, thoughts about plants and quotations from articles and books.

Well, you may say, you could feed this kind of information into the computer, but a personal book in your own handwriting brings back memories more vividly than the typed page. I like to walk round the garden with notebook in hand and later to put my thoughts into my diary. Noting down impressions as they occur is tremendously helpful to beginners, such as I was in 1962, and it also serves to develop your memory as you yourself develop as a gardener. As I look back I realize how some plants, treasured at the time, have disappeared, and I appreciate how fast or how slowly trees and shrubs have grown. As well as making entries about your own garden, you should always take a notebook when you visit other gardens and jot down the special associations of textures and colours which you want to remember. Notes made after visiting nurseries and studying catalogues are important too.

Reading this record over the years, you will discover how your own attitude has matured and your knowledge increased – but also how, sometimes, the imagination of the unsophisticated gardener can be fresher than the disciplined ideas of the garden designer. Simplicity may be best.

I have recorded memories of the late Nancy Lindsay's plants at Sutton Courtenay in Oxfordshire and of Filoli garden in California; of my first visit to Sezincote in Gloucestershire when the stream garden planting had a profound effect on me, and of a memorable summer evening talking to Mr Chick, head gardener at Pyrford Court near Guildford, a garden designed by Gertrude Jekyll. Now I have these memories, and many others, to inspire me when drawing up a garden plan.

With your notebook and camera in hand you can broaden your knowledge of garden planning, noticing how the architectural structure often dictates the planting. The texture of paths is important as well as their siting. Bricks and gravel combine well, and bricks can be laid in geometric patterns. By introducing a difference of levels, with raised beds, a sunken lawn, even a few steps, a flat garden is given a whole new interest. Never forget the third dimension, height, and how you can introduce this with walls, arches, pergolas, trellis and pyramids. Write notes on ideas for climbers and other shrubs to soften and clothe these.

Your book of days will be a practical as well as an inspirational help. Bulb records are among the most useful to keep over the years. Start with the autumn order, including price and provenance, with columns for where and when planted. For good measure you should note their performance and, more important, whether they

Oriental poppies make bright accents
in a mainly blue border at Barnsley House

have been left *in situ* or dug and stored ready for next autumn's planting. Do try to include some new species and varieties as well as the old favourites. Moments spent on your bulb order are vital – they will be reflected in your borders next spring.

We have two different systems. There are the places where bulbs will remain undisturbed for years – under the shrubs and trees, and growing beside hostas, whose leaves will later hide their fading foliage. The small bulbs – *Iris reticulata* and species crocus – are best on the corners of your borders or round the edges where you can enjoy them at close quarters, and where, later in the year, there will be half-hardy annuals, nasturtiums or marigolds.

It is good to have certain parts of the borders where tulips can be bedded out with forget-me-nots or wallflowers, so our second method is to dig and store these for next year's display. When they are in flower, take photographs of them for the record; it helps you to be consistent with your colours. Choose bright days to make photographic records. Some of our borders have white and pink tulips, another always has yellow, and tucked further away are the bright reds. Later, penstemons or salvias or annual tobacco plants, cosmos and larkspur will take their place.

I believe that each season has its own special colours and tones. Early spring is yellow with crocus, narcissus and forsythia, and white and pink with tree blossoms. Midsummer is a luxuriance of pinks, greys and blue. July holds all the colours of the rainbow, and autumn shades move into the rich tones of deep reds, mahogany, orange and bright yellow. This leaves the browns and greens of winter to contrast with blue skies and merge into the frosty days of December and January. How exciting it is to walk round and see the hellebores braving the cold and the first bulbs pushing through.

It is this never-ending cycle, from one season to the next, from one flush of colour to the next, from one surprise to the next, that makes me want to go on gardening. In the garden there is always next season, next year to anticipate. A few snowdrops will multiply into a whole drift, a cutting from a friend's garden may grow into an important feature.

The more you are aware of the changing beauty of your garden each month, the richer your diary will become. It will be absorbing to write and fun to re-read.

Rosemary Verey

A fragrant corner of Philip Watson's Washington Gardens
in Fredricksburg, Virginia

JANUARY

It is good to get back into the garden after the Christmas break. January days are lengthening and the whole gardening year is before me. My New Year's resolution is to notice and appreciate all the good things in the garden – the things that happen by chance, like light falling on tree trunks and long shadows when the sun is low. Now I must take time to see the bulbs pushing through and hellebores opening, and to enjoy the shrubs in bloom.

January, in my garden, is the planning month, a time to think about infilling for borders, to make sure we will have a succession of vegetables, to tackle untidy places and start new projects. We lay and repair paths, and protect new cement from frost. The lily pond needs to be cleaned out every three or four years. With all our walls, we must watch out for mice and set traps, especially where young shoots of bulbs are coming through. I am reminded of John Evelyn, who wrote in his *Kalendarium Hortense* in 1664: 'Set up your traps for vermine; especially in your nurseries of kernels and stones, and amongst your bulbous roots; which will now be in danger.'

On a sunny day, it is rewarding to get out with secateurs, long-handled pruners, gardening steps and a ladder. We prune out crossing branches, shape shrubs to fit their situation, and generally discipline them. We add more vine eyes and crosswires to our walls – we know we will be glad of these in summer – and finish pruning and tying in the wall shrubs. Clematis that flower in late summer on new wood must be pruned now.

If heavy snow comes, a priority is to shake it off the evergreens and to sweep paths to the front door and the garage and greenhouse. The potting shed will certainly need attention and garden seats a scrub. Tools need attention too – we sharpen and repair any that need it and take our mower to be serviced. Frosty days are spent bringing in and cleaning pots and seed trays and looking through weed killers, insecticides and fertilizers, disposing safely of any which are old and probably inefficient. We then make a list of things we need, including sowing compost, trays, bamboos and string. Frames and greenhouse doors often need repair.

Another job I really enjoy is sorting the seeds we collected and put into envelopes last autumn. We store these in an old fridge.

In the vegetable garden, there should still be plenty of Brussels sprouts, leeks, Savoy cabbages, corn salad, parsnips, winter radish and red cabbage to use.

We buy onion sets and put them in trays to develop roots. We find that leeks are an important vegetable for winter, more versatile than onions, so we aim at having early and late season varieties. Names in seed catalogues vary, but we plant 'Autumn Mammoth Snow Star' and 'Autumn Mammoth Startrack', which can be harvested from autumn to midwinter, and for winter use 'Giant Winter-Catalina', sown outside in March and April.

Box balls lining a brick path make interesting winter patterns
at Barnsley House

A) "the spiritual life of abraham Lincoln" —

Week 1

Week 2

A carpet of snowdrops and aconites at Wyck Place,
near Alton in Hampshire

B

Week 3

Week 4

Snow and ice transform the garden
at Hever Castle in Kent

FEBRUARY

The four weeks of February are – paradoxically in view of the weather – a golden time, when the garden need not be demanding. For keen skiers (and gardeners) these are the best weeks to be away. If you stay at home you can choose between reading about plants, making plans and dreaming up ideas, or getting on with your indoor seed-sowing and keeping abreast of outside work. The garden never stops working for you – much is being done underground, as roots and shoots of herbaceous plants develop, and buds begin to swell on deciduous shrubs.

Indoor seed sowing now starts in earnest: we sow in a tray a first batch of sweet peas and manure the ground where these will be planted out. We sow a few hardy annuals like lavateras and rudbeckias, but always remember that our greenhouse will be bursting at the seams in May, waiting for plants to be hardened off.

Outside, we keep weeding and tidying the borders – it is much quicker to pull up or hoe young seedlings than to remove mature weeds. We make sure all our climbers are pruned and tied into the walls and fences, leaving a few spare ties on the wires, handy to use when needed at any time we are walking round the garden.

The grass may be growing, so we look to our lawn fertilizers and selective weed-killers and make sure the mower has had its service. If we are troubled by rabbits or moles, we try to get rid of them now – this is breeding time – and keep our mousetraps baited.

We make sure all our shrubs are fully pruned and that work on ornamental trees and roses is complete. Later in the month we cut back the buddleias severely. This is important or they will become leggy and flower with their heads too high in the air. We winter prune apples and pears too, but remember to enjoy the bulbs which are pushing through.

Inside, we water and fertilize plants in the greenhouse – as the days lengthen, growth begins again. Whitefly will already be trying to take over; now is the moment to suppress them, so get a supply of yellow fly-papers to hang in your greenhouse and conservatory. We find it is helpful to have a spraying programme – for example every Monday or Saturday morning – and alternate the brand.

Geraniums and other cuttings taken last autumn will have rooted and can be potted on. Fuchsias will be making new growth; we use the best shoots for cuttings, then prune hard back to keep the plants compact and shapely, topping up their pots with new compost and watering with Phostrogen to promote new growth.

There is plenty to do in the vegetable garden. We buy early seed potatoes as soon as they are in the shops, and put them out in trays in the light to chit. The lettuce and cauliflower seedlings sown in January can now be planted out under cloches or clear perforated polythene. Lettuce will mature and be harvested first, so can be staggered between the cauliflowers.

A crimson haze of young growth on the avenue of limes
at Barnsley House

Week 1

Week 2

For scent and colour, *Viburnum × bodnantense* 'Dawn'
is one of the best winter-flowering shrubs

Week 3

11-16

Dimitri Orloff: Sleuthing technology
(Technosphere)

Dan Millman

Week 4

Hellebores and pulmonaria carpet the ground
at the Old Rectory, Burghfield in Berkshire

MARCH

March is full of promise, with spring in sight – buds will be swelling and bulbs pushing through everywhere. The early-flowering narcissus species and miniatures ('Tête-à-Tête', 'Peeping Tom', 'Jack Snipe'), as well as the scillas, chionodoxas and *Iris reticulata*, are the reward for our autumn planting.

We enjoy our shrubs as they flower – *Viburnum* × *bodnantense* 'Dawn', *Spiraea thunbergii*, sarcococca, forsythia, chaenomeles, hamamelis, mahonia, osmanthus, *Cornus mas*. I have a huge camellia in a tub by my front door. Spring perennials are flowering too – bergenias, aubrieta, primroses – and the hellebores go on.

But we must keep up with the work, pruning santolinas, artemisias, sage, rue and other grey sub-shrubs to keep them shapely. Lavender, like all 'greys', is better pruned in spring – last year's wood will have protected any precocious young growth in winter. The rue and sage prunings will be used as hardwood cuttings.

The red twigs on the top of the limes – a special winter sight – must be clipped, and the laburnum tunnel pruned and all possible stems tied in. The flower buds will soon be showing. *Cornus sibirica* and *Salix alba* varieties are cut hard back to ensure that the new growth is vigorous and well-coloured.

Feed all your clematis with 50g/2oz of general fertilizer – March is a good month to plant more clematis.

We think about annuals for summer borders and sow seeds of these: *Lavatera* 'Mont Blanc' and 'Silver Cup', *Salvia patens*, cosmos, *Rudbeckia* 'Marmalade', nicotiana in variety, and other favourites. Annual climbers are important too – sweet peas, *Tropaeolum peregrinum*, maurandya, eccremocarpus.

It is exciting when seeds germinate, and even better when they make their show in summer and autumn. We are careful not to sow more seed than we have space for in our frames and greenhouse, remembering that the 'aftercare' is all-important, for a set-back for seedlings will probably be reflected in their eventual performance. We keep a daily watch on them, and look out now and in April for the cyclamen and hellebore seedlings which will be germinating thickly in the garden under the parent plants. We allow some to naturalize and pot up others. They will come in every shade from white to deep burgundy.

On rainy days we sieve and bag up soil from our compost heaps ready for use.

In the vegetable garden we manure the raspberries and put straw round the strawberry plants, covering a few with cloches, to ripen early. We plant out new asparagus plants, cauliflowers, Jerusalem artichokes, shallots, lettuce, early potatoes, and give a nitrogen feed to the brassicas. We plant out our onion sets.

We sow seeds of broad beans, beetroot, Brussels sprouts, cabbage, calabrese, carrots, leeks, parsnips, peas and spinach.

Magnolia stellata makes a cloud of fragrant blossom
at Byways, Burley in Hampshire

Elliot van peshi' 4840 (pruning)

Week 1

Week 2

Iris reticulata pushing through low-growing *Euphorbia myrsinites*
at the Old Rectory, Burghfield in Berkshire

Week 3

Week 4

Grape hyacinths make a ribbon of blue in a border
at Chenies Manor in Buckinghamshire

APRIL

Much of the joy of gardening is in the mind, but April flowers become the reality. Every day brings a fresh surprise – another daffodil or tulip has opened, and it is exciting to discover the beauty of the new varieties we planted last autumn. The camera is in constant use!

Snakeshead fritillaries are at their best, grown both in grass and the borders. They combine well with autumn-flowering cyclamen and lilies. Hyacinths used for forcing a year ago and planted out last autumn will be scenting the garden; they look best in tubs near the house.

A huge boxful of *Leucojum aestivum* (Loddon lily) bulbs, straight from the banks of the Loddon River, were given to us as a present years ago. These pure white summer snowflakes (they actually flower in spring), with green tips to each petal, have increased hugely over the years and I always look forward to seeing their pendant, elegant flowers. The flowers of the white honesty echo the white of the lilies. There are masses of primroses, polyanthus and hellebores, but we always need more to create a natural but worthwhile impact.

There are yellow tulips under *Gleditsia triacanthos* 'Sunburst' and *Narcissus* 'Trevithian' in full flower round the golden privet. Another attractive combination which has worked well are the chionodoxas besides an edging of *Pulmonaria officinalis*.

While we are tidying the borders we keep a look-out for greenfly – especially vulnerable are the leaves of clematis, roses, camellias, evergreen magnolias and honeysuckles, and the flowers of hellebores. We spray these at once.

It is surprising how quickly the look of your borders improves with dead-heading from now right through until autumn – in fact narcissi and tulips will need daily attention. Now is the time to remove the old flower heads of *Hydrangea macrophylla* varieties, carefully cutting to a pair of fat buds. Some stems of *Euphorbia amygdaloides* var. *robbiae* and *E. characias* may have been caught by the frost and so we cut them down to allow new shoots to develop for next year. Penstemons often suffer too and should be pruned to new young growth.

By April we realize what an important part the lawn plays in creating the whole picture. Feeding must not be forgotten: if you want your lawn to be green and healthy you must put back into it the equivalent of what you take out by regular mowing. We try to keep the edges of the grass neatly clipped – this gives the garden that little extra tidy look.

We sow lettuce seed little but often and keep abreast of staking peas and beans. Under glass we sow cucumbers, melons, a few marrows, globe artichokes and runner beans. I enjoy making patterns with the leaves of beetroot, carrots and lettuce, and we sow spring broccoli, curly kale and leeks in a seed bed. This is the month for harvesting rhubarb and asparagus.

Blue and white *Anemone blanda* in a natural setting
at Abbotswood in Gloucestershire

Week 1

Week 2

The yellow crown imperial, *Fritillaria imperialis* 'Maxima Lutea',
makes a dramatic display in the spring

Week 3

Week 4

The hanging heads of snakeshead fritillaries echo those of
Narcissus cyclamineus in a delicate spring planting

MAY

The garden in May is full of colour, sparkling and fresh, with tulips, peonies, aubrieta and spiraea, while hosta leaves are unfolding and ferns unfurling. Excitement is everywhere.

Garden visitors want to discuss what will replace the bulbs. I tell them it will be penstemon of all colours – except yellow! – the annual cosmos, tobaccos and lavateras we grew from seed in January and February, now shouting to be planted out in a richly manured place.

By the end of May, bulbs and spring-flowering shrubs are gently giving way to June roses, clematis, and the young growth of herbaceous plants that evolves into a continuous opening of flowers. But in May we are still concerned with deciding what to do with the fading bulbs. In the four parterre beds near the house, the tulips we grow through forget-me-nots are dug up and put in trays to die down naturally; the ground they have left is then dug over and prepared for the summer display.

Twenty years ago, in early May, we came home from the West Country having seen amazing rhododendrons, magnolias and other spring flowers in bloom, and I had the immediate reaction that my garden needs only soft colours in spring. So we picked all the red tulips near the house and round the pond and laid them on the ground under the laburnums, where they felt wanted and looked at home. That autumn, we planted the bulbs under the trees and in a nearby border put more red tulips, intermixed with yellows – somehow this works, so we have kept the same idea ever since.

The wall climbers will be sending out long new arms, and time must be spent tying these in properly.

May is inevitably a busy time, but I like a day off for the Chelsea Flower Show. It is essential to have a purpose in mind – one year I was looking for golden-leaved shrubs, another for peonies, another for ground cover. Catalogues, heavily marked, will bulge from my bag, to be filed at home.

The moment comes, usually at the end of May, when the lime walk trees must have a clipping. This is done with electric clippers and the clearing-up of the leaves probably takes longer than the actual clipping. We have long pieces of polythene sheet which are kept for laying on the ground to catch the clippings and the final tidy is done with our old vacuuming machine, the 'Billy Goat'. Then there are the box bushes and the threads in the knot garden and herb bed to attend to. We do this by hand and it takes a long time, but the difference before and after is wonderful.

May sees the beginning of culinary bounty. Peas, broad beans, lettuce, young spinach and carrots will all be arriving on the kitchen table and the asparagus will be at its most succulent.

Marrows, courgettes and sweetcorn plants gradually hardened off can go out – but have protection handy in case frost threatens.

A riot of pinks, mauves and yellows in a border
at Barnsley House

Week 1

Week 2

The young leaves of *Philadelphus coronarius*
provide a foil for pastel-hued tulips

Week 3

Week 4

Malus 'Golden Hornet' underplanted with
yellow tulips in Chelmsford, Essex

JUNE

We are always open for the National Gardens Scheme on the first Saturday in June, when the laburnum will be at its best, and this brings lots of visitors. Most of the people who come are keen gardeners, interested both in the layout of the garden and the plants we grow and sell.

Other visitors are surprised that there is not more colour in the borders, unaware that early June is a changeover time: bulbs are over and herbaceous plants and annuals are not yet in flower. We rely on the impact of the rock rose path and the laburnum tunnel. Only once has this let us down, when a severe frost just before Chelsea week froze all the young flower tassels – they just fell off. *Allium aflatunense* carpets the beds under the laburnum and the two colours – yellow and pale mauve – complement each other perfectly.

The changeover involves pulling up forget-me-nots, digging polyanthus and cowslips and lining them out in the vegetable garden to grow on for next season. The tulip bulbs growing with them will be dug, then allowed to die down before storing. In their place will go penstemons, pelargonium and the annuals – cleome, cosmos, nicotianas and *Lavatera* 'Mont Blanc' and others.

A week or so later the borders will be ablaze with colour. Jacob's ladder are everywhere, the red *Paeonia delavayi* smell gorgeous, aquilegias (they seed themselves) look entrancing pushing through grey *Stachys byzantina* and *Geranium pratense*. Lilacs are blooming and so is *Choisya ternata*. *Iris sibirica* round the pond are opening and blend with the nearby *Buddleja alternifolia*. On the house the wisteria looks magnificent, and the thornless *Rosa* 'Zéphirine Drouhin' blooms fresh and sweetly scented.

I like it when a visitor tells me knowingly that the yellow *Meconopsis cambrica* is a weed. Ours have seeded in difficult places and now we have some which are orange and others with double flowers. I love them.

We try to label all the unusual and showy plants – *Asphodeline lutea*, *Dictamnus albus* and *D. albus* var. *purpureus*, the climbing *Actinidia kolomikta* with its striking green, pink and cream-coloured leaves.

We start to clip box around June 1st. The knot must be trimmed by hand but the larger bushes have developed artistic shapes, partly through old age – probably they were planted around 1830 – and partly because lorries often back into them without due care.

June brings the trilogy of roses, strawberries and garden peas – a lovely basketful – and all may be grown in the vegetable garden. I like standard roses to give permanent height. Strawberries can have a bed of their own or be used as an edging. Peas occupy a lot of space and time, but they give us several delicious meals and provide nitrogen for the next crop – brassicas.

To our May bounty we can add globe artichokes, young potatoes, beetroot, courgettes, more varied salads and spring onions.

Yellow laburnums, mauve wisteria and pale purple *Allium aflatunense*
make a tapestry of complementary colours at Barnsley House

Week 1

Week 2

The pink poppy *Meconopsis napaulensis*
brightens the early summer garden

Week 3

Week 4

Culinary bounty in the potager
at Barnsley House

JULY

This is the time to see the garden in the early morning when the light is clear. The herbaceous borders look full and exciting – older and more mature than they were in June, just as beautiful but in a different way. June freshness has turned to July voluptuousness.

Grey foliage is at its best – in the front of the border *Artemisia* 'Powis Castle', *A. stelleriana* and *A. canescens* are a foil for the pinks, mauves, blues and yellows of diascias, felicias, *Viola cornuta* and *V.* 'Belmont Blue', and *Anthemis tinctoria* 'E C Buxton'. *Spiraea japonica* 'Little Princess', with its crimson-rose flower heads, make a round tump in contrast to the spikes of *Salvia nemorosa* 'East Friesland' and the heads of *Allium cernuum*. Penstemon, which we planted in sizeable groups in May and June, are quiet but colourful and will flower for weeks.

We keep staking to a minimum, hoping that our plants are close enough together to hold each other up – but of course there are exceptions. If the delphiniums have grown tall they may well need individual bamboos, put in tactfully to be almost invisible. The tall campanulas, *C. pyramidalis*, *C. lactiflora*, *C.* 'Loddon Anna' and *C. lactifolia*, appreciate a few branching sticks for support. The heavy spikes of *Acanthus spinosus* and *A. mollis* are dramatic in flower and seed-head well into autumn, so warrant individual support. Add all these when the herbaceous material is growing well, so they are never too obvious. A forest of sticks or bamboos from spring until midsummer may be traditional gardening, but I would much rather have a few untidy floppy stems – they seem more natural.

Essentially we like to keep the ground well covered – it seems a waste of opportunity to have bare soil. Dean Hole wrote a century ago that to keep a large garden well stocked you should carry on propagating. This is what inspired me to set up a mist propagator in 1964, which in turn led to our selling surplus plants. Now the selling yard has become a hive of activity.

July is pruning time for the shrubs that flower on the wood they made the previous year – weigela, kolkwitzia, philadelphus, *Spiraea* 'Arguta' and *S.* × *vanhouttei*, deutzia. We take out many of the flowering stems, cutting to strong new shoots which will grow into next year's flowering stems. Summer pruning of roses consists of glorified dead-heading. The standard hawthorn balls, the double red crataegus lining one end of the vegetable garden, are clipped this month to allow them plenty of time to put on new growth and flower buds for next year.

Globe artichokes look attractive in the potager, but must be eaten at the right moment – we have discovered this by trial and error. Later sown broad beans will be ready, and so will the dwarf French. It will be hard to keep up with the courgettes, but we pick them (and give them away) to ensure new flowers. Some cabbages, cauliflowers and Swiss and ruby chard will be ready.

Arches clothed with fragrant roses and a path edged with lavender
at the Old Rectory in Sudborough, Northamptonshire

Week 1

Week 2

Flowers grow in profusion in the Hubbards' seaside garden
at Chilcombe in Dorset

Week 3

Week 4

A corner of the white border at Chenies Manor
in Buckinghamshire

AUGUST

Every year I promise myself visits to other gardens and nurseries, and by August I realize I have only half kept my promise. It is vitally important for one's imagination to be recharged by other ideas and successful planting schemes – and to photograph or jot these down. I have been to Great Dixter in Sussex and Sissinghurst in Kent and admired their hydrangeas, late clematis and other goodies in August and September, but so far have missed their spring bulbs and borders.

The flurry of seed sowing is over and plants have settled into slower routine growth, which sustains their luxuriance. Many are putting on a fine show – herbaceous monardas, astrantias, malvas, hollyhocks and helianthus – but I feel in a holiday mood, like the visitors to our garden.

My diaries remind me that, although dead-heading is vital to keep the borders well dressed, we must allow some flower heads to develop and set seed. The joy of gathering our own lies in the sheer quantity we can collect. We will sow some in our seed bed as soon as they ripen, and keep enough back to sow in trays in spring. Generally those which germinate outside in autumn reach flowering size sooner than those sown indoors in spring.

It is easy to increase your stock of plants with hardwood cuttings. We have a bed on the north-west side of a wall where we start lining out the cuttings in August. Typical examples are spiraea, weigela, rue, lavender, rosemary, hebes, cornus and willows.

Many seeds will be ripening now. We find the easiest way to collect them is to clip the whole seed-head and drop it into a shoe-box or paper bag. The seeds will fall out of their own accord when they are ripe.

On August 20th in 1986, I listed 96 species in flower. The most interesting were *Clematis × durandii*, *Francoa ramosa* and *F. r. alba*, *Rehmannia elata*, *Lysimachia ephemerum*, *Belamcanda chinensis* from Atlanta, Georgia, and a wonderful, very pale yellow hollyhock from France; and the most showy *Aster amellus* 'King George', *Lavatera* 'Barnsley', *Salvia uliginosa* (a wonderful pale blue), *Clematis viticella* 'Purpurea Plena Elegans' and *Heuchera micrantha* 'Palace Purple' (then relatively new in England).

In the vegetable garden, we choose a dry spell to pull the onions and lay them to dry completely before plaiting them. We summer prune the trained apples as soon as the terminal leaf on this year's growth has developed fully, cutting them to two strong buds.

Victoria plums and figs will start to ripen. The last of the globe artichokes are ready, and so are the dwarf French beans. There are quantities of runner beans to pick and some cabbages and cauliflowers. Marrows and courgettes will go on until frost if we keep picking them, but by now the trailing marrows we have trained up the arches are huge and hanging down dramatically. Spinach goes on growing and benefits from picking. The sweetcorn should be ripening – cut and cook them immediately.

A wide herbaceous border in full summer glory
at Bradenham Hall in Norfolk

Week 1

Week 2

Papaver nudicaule lights up the border
at Malleny in Midlothian

Week 3

Week 4

Broad sweeps of pennisetum and other grasses are a feature of this coastal garden
in Chesapeake Bay, Maryland, designed by Oehme, van Sweden and Associates

SEPTEMBER

In September, autumn begins to encroach upon the garden, but in a gentle, well-meaning manner. The yellow helianthus and auburn-coloured heleniums are forerunners of the changing autumn leaves – gold of ginkgo and scarlet of sorbus. Gone is the glare of summer sun, even the shadows are softer, and instead of seeking shade I stand with the warmth of the sun on my back. Suddenly the autumn crocus surprise me as they appear through the rough grass. The spiders' webs, outlined by early morning mist and dew, decorate the evergreens and sometimes a long thread will hang from one tree to the next; as I walk down a path I break this and feel it weaving on my face.

The work we do is mostly tidying – dead-heading. By the end of the month the conkers (fruits of the horse chestnut to my American friends) will start falling and must be kept swept from the drive, or they will squash and stain. The yew hedges have their annual clip with the electric clippers, and afterwards the beech hedge has its trim. Lawn-mowing slows down now but should not be neglected. It is the time to start new borders and a goodly supply of manure and compost must be dug in.

There are two jobs I really enjoy. One is collecting the jet black seeds of *Paeonia delavayi* and sowing these thickly in large trays. They will germinate slowly, sending down a root before making any top growth – then when they are visibly moving they are potted individually. The other job is replanting the tubs. All summer they had held geraniums of all sorts and helichrysum. Now for winter there will be a central evergreen feature – holly usually – surrounded with violas, vincas and heathers and underplanted with bulbs: tulips, daffodils, crocus and *Iris reticulata*. To make a good show next spring we need to plant the bulbs thickly and in layers.

Wasps feeding on our apples are a sure indication that they are ready, and if when you gently cup and lift one it comes away, all is well – you must not cheat and twist. There will be windfalls by now waiting in the grass. Our first crop are 'Laxton's Fortune', beautiful to see and sweet to taste. 'Sunset', 'Tydeman's Late Orange', 'Bountiful' and 'Fiesta' soon to follow. These are carefully stored and so are the Coxes and the Bramleys for cooking.

This is the month when everything you have for lunch can have come from the garden: runner beans and dwarf French, beetroot, carrots and calabrese, celery, corn salad and lettuce, more marrows and courgettes and your own fresh onions, spinach and ruby chard and the last of the sweet corn. Herbs with the salad and chopped with the vegetables make a herby meal.

September is filled with quiet activity – the bees are still out working by day and the Natterer bats skim silently over the pool in late evening. Swallows are busy exercising their wings before their long flight and the Little Owl calls from the darkness. They are all preparing for winter.

Standard roses and sweet peas provide welcome colour
in the potager at Barnsley House

Week 1

Week 2

Late summer profusion, planted by Gary Keim, in Peter Wooster's garden
at Roxbury, Connecticut

Week 3

Week 4

An old stone seat against a tangle of foliage
at Hadspen House in Somerset

OCTOBER

I love working in the garden in October: the feeling of urgency and the festive mood of summer are over and at last we can relax, enjoying days of 'Indian Summer', when the sun shines, and you know – maybe self-indulgently – that those new bulbs can wait a few more days before you plant them. Half-hardy favourites (argyranthemums, felicias and scented-leaved geraniums) can be put indoors in their pots so that they stay in good condition, allowing you to take more cuttings.

So what do we do in October? We clip the hollies and tidy the mixed borders, making the most of the late-flowering perennials and allowing the attractive seed-heads a place of importance. The yellow star-like flowers of *Asphodeline lutea* which graced the June borders are now almost as attractive, their round seed-pods looking like green cherries and eventually turning brown and exploding as the seeds ripen.

We try to make the borders last as long as possible, but must not get behindhand with the routine jobs. The leaf-mould rotted down from last autumn is put into polythene bags, ready for mulching. We weed the lines of perennials and other seedlings sown during the summer.

Before the end of the month we start tidying the borders in earnest. Bulb-planting dictates the timing and order of this. The places for new bulbs are prepared; this involves taking out all the summer bedders. We keep to a pattern of colour throughout the borders. Early narcissus and yellow tulips flower close to *Euphorbia amygdaloides* var. *robbiae*. Another border always has white tulips, and another the pink lily-flowered tulip 'Mariette' with a dwarf prunus.

Some bulbs are left in place – the large-flowered Dutch crocus, for instance, are best planted in a mass down the centres of the borders. The miniature daffodils are important too, and have increased gratifyingly over the years. We try new varieties each year, noting where we put them.

October is apple harvest time, and the apples must be stored safely in a cool atmosphere. They need to be looked over regularly and any bad ones removed. We examine daily the pears already picked and stored – they must be eaten in prime ripe condition, which lasts only one or two days. We pick quinces and grapes for making jelly.

October fruit and vegetables fill our baskets. We harvest and store courgettes and marrows, beetroot, carrots, celeriac, kohl rabi, parsnips, swedes, and pick cauliflowers, calabrese, spinach beet and Brussels sprouts.

Tall varieties of Brussels sprouts are better staked. We give the asparagus bed a generous dressing of manure or compost after cutting down the old stems. Any remaining peas and beans are cut down, leaving their roots, as these produce nitrogen nodules, good for next year's brassicas.

It is essential to start digging. We incorporate manure in areas allocated to next year's peas and beans.

The mixed borders in autumn at Stonecrop,
Frank Cabot's garden in New York State

Week 1

Week 2

Trumpet-shaped flowers of *Brugmansia* 'Charles Grimaldi'
make a focal point in Peter Wooster's Connecticut garden

Week 3

Week 4

When the leaves turn on the lime trees,
autumn has arrived at Barnsley House

NOVEMBER

November can be one of the busiest months, and since I gave up hunting 25 years ago, there has been more time for keeping the garden tidy and preparing for winter. But our energy and thoughts are focused on next year, as we finish the bulb planting, put all the tender plants we want to overwinter inside, take final cuttings of our favourite penstemons, verbena etc, at the same time improving the borders for next summer's look.

I hate to cut down stems of herbaceous plants too soon but my philosophy is to have the borders ready for winter by Christmas time. I like to combine a variety of bulbs among the shrubs and herbaceous plants and these should be in the ground by the end of November. Tulips look good coming through wallflowers and forget-me-nots, and we tuck chionodoxas and scillas under deciduous shrubs where they can remain undisturbed and multiply.

We keep tulips of the same colour to each border every year and so avoid clashes. We label as we plant, and a mulch of leaf mould is the final touch. I am constantly reminded how plants respond to ample feeding. We add our final mulching and feeding in December after the borders are all tidy. We continue to collect seeds from annuals and perennials (see August).

Some years the borders will need more attention and replanning than others, but most herbaceous plants respond well to being divided every two or three years and replanted. We combine this with adding a generous supply of manure or compost. If we dug, divided and lined out our polyanthus after they flowered, they must now go back into the borders, and the cowslips and primroses raised from seed are added too. The nigella we grew in pots from seed sown in August will be ready to plant out, and so will pansies, violas, hellebores and any herbaceous things we have in waiting. It gives me much satisfaction to see the borders well filled at this time of year. Autumn care will be well repaid next spring.

Leaves will be falling all the month and need clearing up. If you allow them to lie on your lawn for too long, the worms will start to drag them in and they will be impossible to rake up. Without our 'Billy Goat' vacuuming machine it would be a long job with rakes. We have two areas of about 3 metres/yards square at the bottom of the garden enclosed with posts and netting, and all the leaves get tipped into one of these. We try to gather them dry when they are light and then water the heap to help the leaves to rot down quickly. They soon heat up and in a year become wonderful leaf mould to be spread on the borders.

There is still a wide selection of vegetables to harvest: Jerusalem artichokes (to store), Brussels sprouts, Savoy cabbage, salsify, Chinese cabbage, lettuce, endive, leeks, winter radish, swedes. Bought lettuces are tasteless now, so we take care to protect our own with cloches, and sow winter lettuce in a frame. We sow seeds of broad beans 'Aquadulce Claudia', having dug in plenty of manure.

A mixed border at Barnsley House made magical
by a November frost

Week 1

Week 2

Among the mountain ashes, *Sorbus* 'Embley' has the best autumn colour
and retains its leaves longer than most

Week 3

Week 4

Box and wall germander form the threads
of the Knot Garden at Barnsley House

DECEMBER

December weather can be capricious – lovely or dramatic, with hard frosts around the middle of the month and snow at Christmas. Work in the garden can be slowing down as the days shorten and Christmas approaches. The gardeners, the garden and I welcome a substantial break. Every year's offering of flowers varies – some years I can pick a bunch of a dozen or more to bring indoors, and sometimes there are enough Christmas roses for the dining-room table and for the crib in church.

After the herbaceous material has finally been cut down, divided and replanted and all bulb planting done, we give a generous mulching of leaf-mould (see October), mushroom compost, manure or other organic material. This feeds, suppresses weeds and looks good. Some herbaceous plants with fleshy roots are better divided in spring.

Working on the walls is always rewarding – and can be more sheltered. We start pruning and tying in our climbing roses and other wall shrubs. Well established ivies will need controlling when they become heavy. We cut back and remove some of the old wood from *Jasminum officinale* and honeysuckles, and take old growth from stephanandra and *Solanum crispum* to encourage the new shoots on which they will flower next summer. When ornamental grapevines have filled their allotted space, we spur prune side shoots to two or three eyes. The Russian vine, *Polygonum baldschuanicum*, should be cut back very hard to the old wood and the golden hop, *Humulus lupulus* var. *aureus*, to the ground – it is herbaceous. At Barnsley, *Itea ilicifolia* and *Garrya elliptica* are grown as wall shrubs, so their loose branches will need to be tied in. We cut buddleias back by one third to have hardwood cuttings from the clippings.

By now all deciduous trees should have shed their leaves, so a final raking-up can be done and the leaf-mould will be maturing, ready to use next autumn.

On wet days there will be greenhouse work to be done. Watering should be reduced and all yellowing leaves removed. We make sure our tender treasures are all under cover. We check that the heating system is in order, clean and firmly fix all the glass panes, and if appropriate line them with bubble plastic to reduce heat loss.

Your Christmas roses will be pushing through and a cloche or a single pane of glass over them will help to keep the petals clean.

New roses should be planted by early December and deciduous shrubs any time during the winter.

There can also be a slowing down of work in the vegetable garden, but greens should be protected from birds with Croptec or netting. Save your best Brussels sprouts for Christmas dinner, and harvest leeks, spinach, red cabbage and salad crops.

Seed catalogues will be on their way and make good fireside reading.

The low winter sun creates long shadows on the grass
at Saling Lodge in Essex

W wellness: eat well — think well and move well — to Be well!

Week 1

Week 2

we 45 ↓ 37% w's - pop 37th last - [illegible] away Medical [illegible]
yet we are ↑ [illegible] key of all [illegible].
Empowering
taking self awareness, self determination, personal responsibility
respect for body to heal self-regulate & adapt to stress

Outlined with rime, a spider's web on *Viburnum tinus*
makes a silvery winter picture

Week 3

Week 4

The scarlet black-eyed berries of *Pyracantha* 'Watereri'
bring a splash of colour in the depths of winter

Angelica archangelica

Date	Nursery	Plant name	Planting position

Date	Nursery	Plant name	Planting position	

Argyranthemum maderense with *Heliotropium* 'Princess Marina'

Date	Nursery	Plant name	Planting position

*Campanula
pyramidalis* var. *alba*

Date	Nursery	Plant name	Planting position

Cardamine pratensis and *Fritillaria meleagris*

Date	Nursery	Plant name	Planting position

Chaenomeles speciosa
'Moerloosei'

Date	Nursery	Plant name	Planting position

Chimonanthus praecox

Date	Nursery	Plant name	Planting position	

Cistus 'Peggy Sammons' with *Diascia rigescens*

Date	Nursery	Plant name	Planting position

Clematis heracleifolia
'Wyevale'

Date	Nursery	Plant name	Planting position

Colchicum autumnale

Date	Nursery	Plant name	Planting position

Cosmos 'Sensation'
and *Lythrum salicaria*
'Firecandle'

Date	Nursery	Plant name	Planting position

Cyclamen persicum

Date	Nursery	Plant name	Planting position

Dahlia 'Bishop of Llandaff' with *Cordyline australis purpurea* and *Crocosmia* 'Lucifer'

Date	Nursery	Plant name	Planting position

Digitalis purpurea alba with *Meconopsis betonicifolia*

Date	Nursery	Plant name	Planting position

Drimys winteri

Date	Nursery	Plant name	Planting position

Eryngium giganteum

Date	Nursery	Plant name	Planting position

Hosta, Foeniculum vulgare and *Sedum*

Date	Nursery	Plant name	Planting position

Gentiana × macaulayi

Date	Nursery	Plant name	Planting position

Geranium psilostemon

Date	Nursery	Plant name	Planting position

Helenium 'Moerheim Beauty' with *Cotinus coggygria* 'Notcutt's Variety'

Date	Nursery	Plant name	Planting position

Hemerocallis
'Missenden' with
heleniums

Date	Nursery	Plant name	Planting position

*Oenothera
missouriensis*

Date	Nursery	Plant name	Planting position

Osteospermum ecklonis
with *Nepeta*

Date	Nursery	Plant name	Planting position

Paeonia lactiflora

Date	Nursery	Plant name	Planting position

Papaver rhoeas and
Calendula officinalis

Date	Nursery	Plant name	Planting position

Potentilla 'Elizabeth'
with *Clematis*
'Hendersonii'

Date	*Nursery*	*Plant name*	*Planting position*

Potentilla 'Gibson's
Scarlet'

Date	Nursery	Plant name	Planting position

Rosa 'Bourbon Queen' with *Hesperis matronalis*

Date	Nursery	Plant name	Planting position

Rosa 'Madame Hardy' and *Aquilegia* McKana hybrids

Date	Nursery	Plant name	Planting position

Verbena rigida with
*Tanacetum
ptarmiciflorum*

Date	Nursery	Plant name	Planting position

Viola 'Huntercombe Purple' with *Allium moly* and *Lysimachia nummularia* 'Aurea'

Photographic Acknowledgments

Geoff Dann both © FLL half-title page, November 2

Jerry Harpur title page, Introduction 2 and 3, January 2 and 3, February 2 and 3, March, May 1 and 3, June 1 and 3, July 1 and 3, August 1 and 3, September 1 and 2, October 1 and 2, December 1 and 3, this page.

Jacqui Hurst both © FLL April 2, May 2

Andrew Lawson Introduction 1, October 3, November 1, © FLL: January 1, February 1, April 1 and 3, August 2, November 3

Michael Warren/Photos Horticultural December 2

Steve Wooster all © FLL June 2, July 2, September 3

Plant portraits all © FLL Geoff Dann, Jacqui Hurst, Andrew Lawson, Marianne Majerus and Steve Wooster

The June garden at Barnsley House